Max & Mila

at the Beach

A fun guide to teaching your child about skin cancer, melanoma and sun safety

Written and Illustrated by
Amalyn Persohn Martin & Jennifer Anne Danker

Written and Illustrated by

Amalyn Persohn Martin & Jennifer Anne Danker

Whale animal designed by Breanna Lilith Graf

Lovingly dedicated to our children

Bailey, Mila, Ethan and Max.

Hello, beach buddies! Meet Mila and Max.

They want to share some sun safety facts!

They notice their friend Colin looks very red.

"Oh my! I think you have a sunburn!" Mila said.

"Sunburn you say? Oh it burns so much!

My shell hurts even with the slightest touch."

Please teach me friends how not to burn.

I'm all ears and am ready to learn!

If you're going to play in the sun or ocean,
make sure you've used the smartest lotion...

Cover yourself with sunscreen from head to toes.
And don't forget your neck, ears and nose!

I promise I will buy sunscreen at the store.

Now Mila, please, please tell me more!

Slide on some sunglasses to shield your eyes.

Wearing a swim or sun shirt is also quite wise.

Protect your head with a hat that's big and wide.

This will shield you from the sun while outside!

Moles are small dark circles on your skin.

They can be on your arms, legs and even chin.

Some are good and some are bad,

But if they change or bleed, tell your mom or dad.

Now that I know how to be safe in the sun,

let's go build a sand castle and have some fun!

Dear Parents and Teachers,

The purpose of this book is to educate your little one about sun safety and most importantly, to continue to use these principles in your everyday lives. Melanoma is thought to occur rarely in children. However, a number of recent publications and our own experience clearly indicate that a profound change in the natural history of melanoma is now occurring and that melanoma, indeed, is occurring much more frequently in children and teenagers. Teaching children healthy habits at a young age and making it as common as teeth brushing and eating three healthy meals a day is imperative.

The best way to prevent melanoma is to minimize exposure of your children's skin to sunlight; the younger they are when they start practicing sun-safe behavior the greater the benefit. A single bad sunburn under the age of 20 may double the risk of melanoma; three blistering sunburns multiplies the risk by five. Minimize exposure from 10 am to 4 pm when the sun is strongest, make sure they wear protective clothing including a wide-brim hat. Sunscreens prevent less serious skin cancers but they won't prevent melanoma if your child stays in the sun for a long time. If you use sunscreen, make sure it is waterproof, has an SPF rating of 30 or more for both UVA and UVB, is applied heavily and is reapplied every 90 minutes or less.

Now is the time to take action to prevent the tragedy of melanoma from affecting your children. The first step is to learn more about it yourself. Please visit www.milesagainstmelanoma5k.org to view their resources and learn more about decreasing your family's risk.

Please tell your friends and family about this book as 10% of each book sale goes towards melanoma research!

Very Best Regards,

Amalyn and Jen

About Amalyn and Miles Against Melanoma

Amalyn was born in Metairie, Louisiana but moved to St. Louis after her father was relocated. This Missouri State straight-A student studied psychology, criminal justice, and child/family development while working four jobs and volunteering at a women's domestic violence shelter, mentoring at risk youth and serving various ranks in organizations on campus, including the President of the Criminal Justice Society. She first served in the public sector at Green County's Courthouse; in Detention and then the Abuse & Neglect Unit. Her last public sector position was as victim's advocate for St. Charles County Courthouse. But with budget cuts looming, Amalyn feared for her family's finances. She was offered a sales job in the private sector and now serves as a Marketing Representative for St. Louis Physical Therapy.

In 2010 she founded Miles Against Melanoma, a registered 501c3 nonprofit to educate the public about melanoma and raise funds for struggling melanoma patients and families. She works full force for this organization voluntarily.

Miles' Message and Vision is as follows:
- To increase awareness of malignant melanoma and skin cancer through education, advocacy and research.
- To advocate for detection and to obtain skin examinations. We help people find dermatologists in their area as well.
- To ease the burden and to provide support for melanoma patients, caregivers and medical professionals through financial aid.
- To create a national association to aid in providing support to those with melanoma.
- To ultimately find a cure for melanoma.

According to Martin, Miles Against Melanoma's goal is to spread to every city in the United States to change the mindset of Americans and bring about community awareness in every state. Thanks to Ms. Martin, Miles Against Melanoma is in over 15 cities. To Amalyn, melanoma is a seemingly underrated and underexposed disease that needs more awareness. If you are interested in having an event in your city, please let her know at milesagainstmelanoma@yahoo.com.

Like all moms, she strives to protect her two children, including protecting them from the dangers of the sun. Seeing families and individuals affected by melanoma is difficult for her which makes her work that much harder to educate others on sun safety. As with anything, reaching people in their prime will have the most profound effect and it is her greatest hope that the values will be instilled in not only her children but in all.

Made in the USA
Lexington, KY
27 August 2014